RABBI
TEACH US TO
PRAY

AARON EBY

WHAT THE
JEWISHNESS OF JESUS
CAN TEACH CHRISTIANS
ABOUT PRAYER

RABBI
TEACH US TO
PRAY

AARON EBY

FIRST FRUITS OF ZION

First Fruits of Zion is a 501(c)(3) registered nonprofit educational organization.

Printed in the United States of America

ISBN: 978-1-941534-25-0

The prayer text in this book, which includes Scriptural passages, is an original translation by the author.

All other Scriptural quotations, unless otherwise noted, are from the Holy Bible, English Standard Version®, copyright © 2001 by Crossway Bibles, a publishing ministry of Good News Publishers. Used by permission. All rights reserved.

Also cited: The New American Standard Bible®, © 1960, 1962, 1963, 1968, 1971, 1972, 1973, 1975, 1977, 1995 by The Lockman Foundation. Used by permission.

Cover design: Avner Wolff

Quantity discounts are available on bulk purchases of this book for educational, fundraising, or event purposes. Special versions or book excerpts to fit specific needs are available from First Fruits of Zion. For more information, contact www.ffoz.org/contact.

First Fruits of Zion

PO Box 649, Marshfield, Missouri 65706–0649 USA
Phone (417) 468–2741, www.ffoz.org

Comments and questions: www.ffoz.org/contact

Contents

Introduction

Prayer in the World of Jesus

What is a disciple?

Discipleship already existed as a well-established institution within Judaism long before the appearance of Jesus and his followers. All the great sages, rabbis, leaders of the Pharisees, and teachers of the Bible had disciples. The Hebrew word for "disciple" is *talmid*, a word that simply means "student." A disciple's job was to learn everything his master had to teach.

The association between disciple and master was much deeper than the typical teacher-student relationship today. Disciples memorized their teachers' interpretations, explanations, and exegesis of Scripture. They memorized the stories, parables, illustrations, and anecdotes their teachers told.

Disciples learned through imitation. They learned to live out the Bible's instructions by mimicking their teachers and incorporating their manner of observance into their own. Disciples kept the commandments the way they learned from their teachers. A disciple endeavored to become like his or her teacher: "A disciple is not above his teacher, but everyone when he is fully trained will be like his teacher" (Luke 6:40).

This explains why Jesus' disciples were so eager to learn from the Lord about prayer:

> Jesus was praying in a certain place, and when he finished, one of his disciples said to him, "Lord, teach us to pray, as John taught his disciples." (Luke 11:1)

Praying is such a natural, simple act. Prayer is talking to God. It is what we were created to do. Is it necessary to study and research something so basic?

Jesus' disciples had grown up as observant Jews; they had been praying all their lives. Nevertheless, they knew that there was more for them to learn, and they wanted to imitate their Master in prayer. While prayer is a simple concept, it is worthy of deep, lifelong study.

We followers of Jesus today also desire to be true disciples. We wish to follow Jesus' teachings, imitate his actions, and let his words flow easily from our lips. We want to pray as he prayed.

Those of us in the Western world face somewhat of a cultural barrier. We follow a Jewish rabbi named Yeshua who lived thousands of years ago in the land of Israel. As artistic depictions throughout the centuries have shown, it is much easier to make Jesus seem like one of us than it is for us to become like him.

Becoming like him does not mean that non-Jewish Christians need become or act like first-century Jews. However, for us to relate Jesus' teachings to our culture and time, we must recognize and understand the Jewish culture that permeates the New Testament. Just as a verse can be taken out of context, so the entire Bible is out of context if it is divorced from the Jewish people.

By the same token, we can gain such a richness and depth by restoring the Jewish context of the Gospels. Like the Jewish people who are returning to the land of Israel and thriving today, it is inspiring to see the words of our Master come alive when they, too, return to their native soil.

Service of the Heart

The Intense Connection between Prayer and Sacrifice

The young man's white linen robe shone in the morning sun; his sharp knife glistened as he bent down to the restrained animal. He paused for a moment; one wrong thought would render this sacrifice useless. Glancing toward the court of Israel, he spotted the man who had sent the animal standing just below the Levitical platform. A burnt offering for the LORD, he thought in his heart, and in a smooth, swift motion, the knife opened the goat's neck.

❖ ❖ ❖

In the ancient Temple the priests performed many duties in connection with the sacrifices and offerings. They slaughtered, flayed, skinned, and butchered animals. Sacred portions went up in smoke on the altar, while the remaining meat was cooked and eaten. In modern Western culture most of us have no qualms about processing meat, but it would seem bizarre and foreign to those in our society to do so as an act of worshiping a deity.

The Heartbeat of the Whole Earth

Christians are most familiar with sacrifices as they relate to sin, atonement, and forgiveness. But the Jewish sacrifices were much more than that. The Hebrew word for sacrifice, *korban*, has the basic meaning of "drawing near." Sometimes this drawing near served as a remedy for the distance between people and God caused by sin or negligence. Other times it was a simple act of love, devotion, or thanks.

The priests had many other duties as well. Removing ashes, hauling firewood, preparing and offering the aromatic incense, and preparing and lighting the lamp stand (called the menorah) are some examples. The Bible describes the sacrifices and other tasks using the Hebrew word *avodah*, which literally means "service" or "work."

Scripture uses this term in other ways as well. Deuteronomy 10:12 reads,

> Now, Israel, what does the LORD your God require of you, but to fear the LORD your God, to walk in all his ways, to love him, to serve the LORD your God with all your heart and with all your soul?

What does it mean to serve God with our hearts? If "service" in the Temple means offering sacrifices, then what type of "service" would we do in our own hearts? The ancient rabbis pondered this question and concluded that the phrase "service of the heart" must refer to prayer.

But wait—does this term suggest that, while prayer is done with heartfelt intention, the sacrificial rituals in the Temple were merely mindless motions? This cannot be since even the sacrifices had to be performed as expressions of sincere love for God and with full concentration. Also, we express prayer with our mouths; we do not merely ponder or feel it in our hearts. So how could prayer be considered service of the heart but sacrifice not be?

The "heart" does not refer to an organ used to perform prayer. Rather, it is the place where the service of God happens. Likewise, the Levitical duties are not the service of the hands; they are the service of the altar.

In the Temple at the time of Jesus, the altar was a massive stone platform. Priests carried golden vessels of blood and splashed some of the blood against the sides of the altar, then poured the remainder into drains at the altar's base. From there the blood flowed out through underground channels into the Kidron Valley, one of Jerusalem's streambeds. The priests ascended the altar by a huge ramp and placed sacred portions of meat on one of the large fires that burned on its top. Ancient Jewish sources reported that the smoke from those sacrifices rose like a pillar into the sky, untouched by the wind.

In some way beyond human understanding, this process caused the presence of God to connect with a physical place on earth. The Tabernacle in the wilderness and, later, the Temple in Jerusalem were spaces where one could encounter the Creator of the universe.

Prayer has the same effect, except instead of drawing the Spirit of God into a courtyard or building, it moves him to take residence inside our hearts.

The correspondence between sacrifice and prayer is remarkable. The daily rhythm of the sacrifices mimics the lub-dub coursing of blood through our hearts but on a monumental scale. The Temple, as it were, is like the beating heart of the whole earth. In the absence of the Temple, this heartbeat nonetheless continues among those who draw near to their Creator in prayer.

LET MY PRAYER BE COUNTED AS INCENSE

Sitting under the open sky in the Temple court, the pale stone platform-like altar was the size of a house. Within the Sanctuary was a much different kind of altar. A little more than waist high, its ornate gold designs enclosed a wooden interior.

Freshly arranged coals glowed atop the golden altar's square surface. An elderly priest stood with his cupped hands full of reddish powder. His colleague stood at the doorway, peering out and waiting for the correct moment. "Burn it!" he called, and then departed, leaving the priest alone in the holy place.

Immediately the old man reached out over the coals and began to let the powder sift through his fingers. He started on the far side, drawing his hands back toward his body so that the rising smoke would not burn them. As the fine dust hit the coals, it billowed and sparked with a crackling noise, sending a pungent, bittersweet fragrance into the air. The hot smoke raced toward the ceiling.

The old man gasped as a humanlike figure to his right caught his eye. "Do not be afraid, Zechariah, for your prayer has been heard."

❖ ❖ ❖

Prayer and sacrifice have strong parallels, but they are not entirely the same. The sacrificial service serves to draw the entire world collectively near to God, so it happens externally in a central location. Prayer connects each individual with our Father in heaven, and this takes place within each one of us.

The two are not interchangeable or redundant. To the contrary, prayer was always to accompany the sacrifice. To sacrifice without sincere prayer would have been pointless and empty.

On the other hand, prayer stands on its own. Even in situations in which sacrifice is not possible, prayer is worthwhile and effective. Prayer is a powerful opportunity to meet with the Creator of the universe in the comfort of our own hearts.

When the Romans destroyed the Temple in 70 CE and the sacrificial services could no longer take place, the leading Jewish voices at that time assured their community that prayers could continue nonetheless. They based this on Hosea 14:3[2]:

> Take words with you, and return to the LORD. Say to him, "Forgive all iniquity, and accept what is good. Let us exchange bulls for our lips." (author's translation)

The Hebrew of this biblical passage is difficult but clever. The word for "exchange" sounds as if it means, "bring a peace offering." The word "bulls" is similar to the word "fruit," making a phrase reminiscent of "the fruit of our lips."

Hosea pleaded with Israel at the time when the Northern Kingdom had fallen into apostasy and was worshiping false gods. The people's sacrifices to God were meaningless because of their unfaithfulness. Hosea explained that the solution was not to offer more empty sacrifices. Rather, he said, "For I desire steadfast love and not sacrifice, the knowledge of God rather than burnt offerings" (Hosea 6:6). Hosea's desire was for the people to repent by turning to God with prayer and changing their ways.

The author of Hebrews also picks up on this theme, comparing words and good deeds to sacrificial offerings:

> Through him then let us continually offer up a sacrifice of praise to God, that is, the fruit of lips that acknowledge his name. Do not neglect to do good and to share what you have, for such sacrifices are pleasing to God. (Hebrews 13:15–16)

King David expressed the connection between the offering of incense and his prayers as well:

> Let my prayer be counted as incense before you, and the lifting up of my hands as the evening sacrifice! (Psalm 141:2)

This theme appears once again in Revelation:

> Another angel came and stood at the altar with a golden censer, and he was given much incense to offer with the prayers of all the saints on the golden altar before the throne, and the smoke of the incense, with the prayers of the saints, rose before God from the hand of the angel. (Revelation 8:3–4)

This spiritual reality should encourage us. Just as the sacrifices were powerful and effective in bringing the presence of the infinite God to our finite earth, so too, prayer draws the Spirit of God into our hearts. However, sacrifice requires elaborate preparation, a sanctified priesthood, and an undefiled environment. How are we to emulate this in prayer, especially when we feel unprepared and unworthy?

The writer of Hebrews gives us hope that the Messiah has already prepared the way, allowing us to engage in prayer—the service of the heart—with confidence and assurance:

> Therefore, brothers, since we have confidence to enter the holy places by the blood of Jesus, by the new and living way that he opened for us through the curtain, that is, through his flesh, and since we have a great priest over the house of God, let us draw near with a true heart in full assurance of faith, with our hearts sprinkled clean from an evil conscience and our bodies washed with pure water. (Hebrews 10:19–22)

Let's not take this opportunity lightly. When we draw near to God in prayer as disciples of Yeshua of Nazareth, we capture the attention of the infinite, all-powerful Being who created us, chose us, and loves us.

CONVERSATION WITH THE CREATOR

EXTEMPORANEOUS PRAYER IN THE JEWISH FAITH

Malka stood in the cool shade of the Western Wall's stones. So many Jewish tears had been shed in this sacred spot that Gentile onlookers had taken to calling it the "Wailing Wall," but to Malka it was the Kotel HaMa'aravi, the ancient retaining wall that had once formed the base of the Holy Temple.

The melodious sound of the morning prayers rung out from the men's section across the divider. Malka held her prayer book near her face, but only to block out the commotion and create a miniature private sanctuary. She poured out her heart to God in her own words.

What she said was not particularly poetic, profound, or well organized, but it certainly was heartfelt. At times she bubbled over with gratitude and love; other times she sounded more like an unsatisfied customer trying to explain why she deserved a full refund. Just about everything came up: her children, her finances, her parents in America, victims of a recent terror attack, her social anxiety, her brother in the Israel Defense Forces, her sister's recent surgery, the elections …

❖ ❖ ❖

P rayer is talking to God. Conversational, extemporaneous prayer is the oldest kind of prayer; it goes all the way back to Adam. Over time poets, prophets, and scholars have composed powerful and inspiring odes, psalms, hymns, and petitions that are treasured by the Jewish community, but they have never lost the art of simple conversation.

Constant Awareness

Jewish life is designed to remind a person of the presence of God. Observant Jewish men wear a skullcap called a *yarmulke*; its name relates to the Hebrew words for "fear of the king," and it serves as a continuous reminder that God is above. Tassels known as *tzitzit* dangle from a four-cornered undershirt; the Bible explains that their purpose is for Jews "to look at and remember all the commandments of the LORD, to do them" (Numbers 15:39).

Before tasting any food, when seeing a rainbow, after hearing thunder, and even after using the bathroom, Jews utter a brief expression of thanks. Many Jews try to be cognizant of even the smallest, most mundane details of life and carry them out in a way that acknowledges the presence of God.

These habits have the potential to make one's whole life feel like a conversation with our Father in heaven. At the very least, it calls to our attention the fact that he is always listening and interested in what we do and say. It reminds us to be full of gratitude for even the basic things in life.

Pray without Ceasing

Scripture instructs us that prayer should be constant in our lives: "Rejoice always, pray without ceasing, give thanks in all circumstances; for this is the will of God in Christ Jesus for you"

(1 Thessalonians 5:16–18). This verse expresses the Jewish attitude toward prayer. When one remains aware of God's presence, all of life becomes a constant conversation with him.

The "constant conversation" mode of Jewish prayer is depicted (albeit somewhat caricatured) in *Fiddler on the Roof* as Tevye freely includes God in his everyday life. While not every observant Jew communicates with God in this manner throughout the day, some certainly do, and this is natural within Jewish life. Mothers with small children may not find many opportunities to complete the formal daily prayers at their set times, but by speaking with God throughout the day, they maintain an intimate connection with him. The ancient sage Rabbi Yochanan said, "Would that a man pray all day long!"

Perhaps we do not feel eloquent enough to pray. But prayer does not require poetry. Our private prayers should be in our native language, in the type of speech that is most natural for us, because it should express what is in our hearts. Our goal is not to impress God with our vocabulary but to open communication with him. We can think of ourselves as small children with our mother or father.

In any case, if we do not have the words to pray, then that is what we should pray about. We should tell our Father in heaven that we can't think of what to say and why. If we feel inadequate or unworthy or overwhelmed, we can tell him that and ask him for help.

Conversational prayer dispels the excuse "I don't have time to pray." We can talk with God in this way while walking, driving, washing dishes, or gardening. Jews do not have the custom of bowing heads or folding hands when praying. Just talking, as when talking to any friend, is good enough.

Wrestling in Prayer

The soil had turned to dust. The children's mouths were parched. The drought had gone on too long, so there was no water for the crowds arriving in Jerusalem for Passover. In desperation the people turned to Honi, a man whose prayers had proven to be effective.

Honi prayed, but no rain fell. Honi then traced a circle in the dust and stepped inside. "I will not move from this place until you have compassion on your children!" he cried out to God.

❖ ❖ ❖

We might feel too distant from God to speak to him. This becomes a self-fulfilling notion, of course. Even if we feel utterly rejected by God, we have to fight back. We have to demand that our Father take us back—and to keep doing so no matter how long it takes. He *wants* us to do this. Prayer, from a Jewish perspective, is a struggle. It is a struggle within ourselves, and it is a struggle with God.

Moses did exactly this when God threatened to reject Israel. He struggled with God and actually won.

After the incident of the golden calf, God told Moses, "Let me alone, that my wrath may burn hot against them and I may consume them, in order that I may make a great nation of you" (Exodus 32:10). But when Moses refused God's order, "the LORD relented from the disaster that he had spoken of bringing on his people" (Exodus 32:14).

How was it possible for Moses to win against the Creator of the universe? It was possible precisely because God wanted him to win. Because Moses was willing to take up the challenge, God gave him the tools to do so.

Ponder this for a moment. Why would God tell Moses to "let him alone" so he could destroy the people? Wasn't God powerful enough to carry out his will regardless of what Moses did?

But read between the lines. In essence, God was hinting to Moses, "If you do not let me alone, my wrath will not burn against them." In other words, "I have granted you the power to intervene and prevent me from carrying out my wrath."

As disciples of Jesus, we can use our connection to him to our advantage. It can become our ultimatum, our trump card, our checkmate. That's what it is for. "I may not be worthy to serve you and experience your love and favor, but I put my trust in your Son, and I cling to him. That means you cannot reject me—you cannot be distant from me without rejecting him! Now take me back, and draw me close to you!"

It sounds audacious. It sounds demanding. In Yiddish we Jews might say it sounds *chutzpadik*. Welcome to the world of Jewish prayer.

Is praying in such a manner appropriate or even permitted? In a sense, standing uninvited before the all-powerful King of all kings should not be permitted at all, let alone setting before him a list of demands! But we should see ourselves like Queen Esther, who barged in before her husband to plead for her life. It is permitted precisely because we have no other choice. Prayer is our lifeline.

This is how Jesus prayed and how he taught us to pray. He instructed us to cry to God day and night, like a widow demanding justice before an unjust judge, harassing him until he relents and grants her request (Luke 18:1–8).

As for Honi in his circle, eventually a faint drizzle began to fall. "I did not ask for this but for water to fill the cisterns!"

The sky broke open, and a destructive rainstorm threatened the land. "I did not ask for this but for rain of favor and blessing!"

A gentle, steady rain began to water the land, just as he had asked.

The other Jewish scholars at the time did not approve of Honi's tactics, but what could they say? "You are like a child who throws a tantrum before his father, and his father does whatever he asks."

Psalms: The Bible's Prayerbook

As the bus pulled away from the station, Malka turned to the back cover of her book of Psalms and retrieved a worn, folded piece of notepaper. Opening it, she glanced over the list of names of loved ones in need of healing. She smiled in gratitude as she noticed how many names had been crossed out. Then she found Psalm 20, on a well-worn page, and began to recite.

The words came out with minimal effort; occasionally she glanced down at the page. Though King David had penned the words, they took on new meaning as she focused her heart on the names from her list.

She concluded with a brief prayer that God would heal each person on her list, bringing restoration to every organ and connection in each one's body as well as complete spiritual restoration. "Thank you, Abba," she uttered with a smile as she stood to exit the bus.

❖ ❖ ❖

From a Jewish perspective, the Scriptures are not just for reference purposes. As the sacred words of God, they deserve in their own right to be studied and read aloud. Reading and studying Scripture is an expression of worship in and of itself. It pleases God to hear his words read aloud to him in an audible, human voice.

The psalms are special in this regard because even though they are God's Word, they are prayers. They are expressed in the voice of humanity. How much more, then, is it appropriate for humans to utter them in prayer! The psalms are a powerful source of guidance. They make it possible for us to pray in alignment with God's will even when words fail us.

In the days of the apostles, the book of Psalms constituted the hymnal of the Levites, who recited its passages in the Temple as a musical accompaniment to the sacrifices. For example, many of the psalms speak of offering a "sacrifice of thanksgiving," which is a category of animal sacrifice outlined in Leviticus 7:11–18. Psalm 100, which is subtitled "A Psalm for giving thanks" (yes, the subtitle is in the original Hebrew text), was one of the psalms that the Levites recited as they offered these animals on the Temple altar.

In Jewish practice, psalms can be selected topically for certain circumstances. However, many Jewish people follow a schedule that allows them to read the entire book of Psalms once a month or even once a week. Sometimes a women's prayer group will divide the chapters among everyone in attendance and team up to recite the entire book in one meeting.

Psalms also make up the bulk of the traditional prayers in the Siddur, the daily prayer book. They serve as expressions of praise, mourning, supplication, thanksgiving, hope, and devotion. Because the psalms occur so frequently as part of the daily prayers, it is common for many observant Jews to have memorized several of them in Hebrew.

The love and intimate familiarity that the first generation of Jesus' followers had for the psalms are apparent in the book of Acts. The prophetic and insightful words of the psalms quickly came to their minds and flowed from their lips.

Christianity inherited the practice of praying the psalms from Judaism through the apostolic community. Many Christians pray through the book of Psalms to this day; this practice is something precious that Christianity and Judaism have shared in common. In earlier generations it was not uncommon for Christians to memorize the entire book of Psalms. Because of its use as a Christian prayer book, the book of Psalms is often bundled together with printed editions of the New Testament.

Part of the love that both Christians and Jews have for the psalms stems from their deep connection with messianic prophecy. King David, the progenitor of the Messiah, wrote many of the psalms. Some are even written in the Messiah's voice.

By virtue of the messianic nature of the psalms, which are in the voice of Messiah and which the Messiah surely prayed, we participate with Jesus in his own prayers. As such, praying the psalms affords us an effectual and transformative opportunity for an intimate connection with Jesus.

To this day the psalms are a powerful arsenal in the hands of Jewish and Christian petitioners. Whether we are in distress, in need of healing or comfort, or overflowing with thanks, the psalms put eloquent words to our thoughts.

SOUNDING AN ALARM

The olive leaves shuddered in the midnight breeze; the full moon's light flickered. The Master lay with his face in the dust, crying out in broken sobs; Peter, James, and John averted their eyes in discomfort. They were still weary from the Passover wine; the aftertaste of the bitter herbs still lingered in their mouths. "My Father, if it be possible, let this cup pass from me; nevertheless, not as I will, but as you will" (Matthew 26:39).

❖　❖　❖

When life presents challenges, our first instinct should be to cry out to God for help. We should not say, "I got myself into this mess; I'll get myself out." Nor should we assume that because God already knows our needs, it is pointless to call on him. We must certainly not say, "I don't deserve to ask God for help now because I did not pray when things were going well." Rather, God is eager to hear the prayers of all those who raise their voices to him and ask him for help.

Many scriptures express this notion, but the ancient rabbis derived it from a surprising source:

> When you go to war in your land against the adversary who oppresses you, then you shall sound an alarm with the trumpets, that you may be remembered before the LORD your God, and you shall be saved from your enemies. (Numbers 10:9)

They noted that before engaging in combat, the Israelites were to "sound an alarm" in order to gain God's attention. This is not talking merely about trumpet blasts but about prayer.

The verse says "that you may be remembered." God is not forgetful or oblivious, so what is the point of such a prayer? It is our acknowledgment that God is in control of outcomes. While we may march forth in battle, through prayer we admit that success and failure are not in our hands, nor are they a matter of chance or fate.

We must never hold an indifferent posture toward God wherein we attribute our trials to mere accidents and coincidence. By doing so, we fail to recognize his supreme control over all things in life.

As such, it is critical that we rush to our Father in prayer at all times of distress, whether our problems are personal or community-wide. We should also examine our lives to make sure that we are carrying out God's will rather than our own:

> He said, "Abba, Father, all things are possible for you. Remove this cup from me. Yet not what I will, but what you will." (Mark 14:36)

We might think that the Son of God would have an easy time getting his wishes fulfilled. Instead we learn,

> In the days of his flesh, Jesus offered up prayers and supplications, with loud cries and tears, to him who was able to save him from death, and he was heard because of his

reverence. Although he was a son, he learned obedience through what he suffered. (Hebrews 5:7–8)

The matriarchs of the Jewish people, Sarah, Rebekah, Rachel, and Leah, were all barren. Why was this so? The ancient rabbis suggested, "Because the blessed Holy One longs for the prayers of the righteous." It is not that God enjoys our suffering, but when we pray in times of difficulty, it has a transformative effect and binds us in closeness to our Creator. Children who are born to barren parents after intense prayer are sure to be raised with special dedication to God.

Receiving a gift from God in answer to fervent prayer, then, is far superior to receiving gratuitous blessings.

THERE IS NO OTHER

When adversity comes, sometimes spiritually inclined people make the mistake of attributing independent power to the devil. While they would not consider the devil to be as strong as God, they seem to put the two on a level playing field by supposing that the Almighty has let an attack sneak by.

From the perspective of Judaism, this would constitute a major error bordering on idolatry. Moses explained to the Israelites,

> To you it was shown, that you might know that the LORD is God; there is no other besides him. Out of heaven he let you hear his voice, that he might discipline you … Know therefore today, and lay it to your heart, that the LORD is God in heaven above and on the earth beneath; there is no other. (Deuteronomy 4:35–39)

Difficulties in our lives are not outside the sovereignty of God; somehow they serve a greater purpose. Occasionally at the end of it all, we can perceive that purpose, but in some cases it is beyond our ability to grasp in this life.

The concept that "there is no other besides him" means that we should not see hardships as outside attacks but as tests that provide us with the opportunity to grow:

> Count it all joy, my brothers, when you meet trials of various kinds, for you know that the testing of your faith produces steadfastness. And let steadfastness have its full effect, that you may be perfect and complete, lacking in nothing. (James 1:2-4)

We might think that if calamity comes to us under the sovereignty of God, then who are we to resist it? By all means, we must resist evil and do whatever we can to alleviate suffering, both through our actions and through prayer. If we find ourselves in a position to work and pray to end suffering, then we are assuredly there "for such a time as this" to involve ourselves in God's process of redemption. Such testing provides opportunities for us to rise to the challenge that our Father has set before us. When we cry out to God, we confess that he alone has the power to change outcomes. There is no other.

THE HOUR OF PRAYER

HOW THE DAILY TIMES OF PRAYER CAN TRANSFORM OUR LIVES

The rugged and seasoned military officer peered westward. From this rooftop in Caesarea, he could not see his homeland in faraway Italy—only the afternoon sunlight that glimmered on the cresting waves. Cornelius turned away and faced the southeast, toward the place the Jews called the "holy city." This was the hour of prayer; it was his chance to lift his voice to the Creator in concert with the smoke of the sacrifices and the songs of the Levites.

Just then, "he saw clearly in a vision an angel of God come in and say to him, 'Cornelius.' And he stared at him in terror and said, 'What is it, Lord?' And he said to him, 'Your prayers and your alms have ascended as a memorial before God'" (Acts 10:3–4).

❖ ❖ ❖

God orchestrated this world with natural rhythm. He declared that the sun, moon, and stars would be "for signs and for seasons, and for days and years" (Genesis 1:14).

The Rhythm of Creation

Some people might not like the idea of God being so predictable. Yet according to Scripture, he made a calendar and filled it with yearly appointments. The Bible lists these festivals (such as Passover and the Day of Atonement) in Leviticus 23. It describes them with the Hebrew word *mo'ed*, which means "appointment" or "meeting." These appointed times both memorialize and rehearse the interactions between God, his people Israel, and the entire world.

On the biblical calendar, the phases of the moon signal the turn of the months. The appearance of the first sliver marks a day of celebration (Numbers 10:10). Likewise, the seventh day of each week is like a sanctuary in time, a day that God set apart and blessed (Genesis 2:3).

In recent years many Christians have begun to participate in these holy days. They find inspiration in the rich messianic symbolism as well as the opportunity to meet with God at the holy times he designated.

The Daily Appointments

Holy times occur not only on a yearly, monthly, or weekly basis. Some appointed times occur every single day:

> The LORD spoke to Moses, saying, "Command the people of Israel and say to them, 'My offering, my food for my food offerings, my pleasing aroma, you shall be careful to offer to me at its appointed time.'" (Numbers 28:1–2)

This passage goes on to describe a burnt offering that was to take place twice each day. Each offering consisted of a lamb, grain, and wine. The priests offered one in the morning as the first sacrifice of the day. The other, the last sacrifice of the day, took place in the afternoon. (Although some Bibles say "twilight" or "evening," "afternoon" is a more accurate interpretation.)

Like the annual festivals, this twice-daily sacrifice was to take place at an "appointed time"; this phrase comes from the same Hebrew word *mo'ed* as before. As the priests were to be "careful" about offering them, the timing of these sacrifices was clearly important to God. In establishing these daily appointed times, God built a rhythm of worship into each day.

As we have noted, there is a close relationship between sacrifice and prayer. As the burnt offerings ascended in smoke to heaven, the Israelites on earth poured out their hearts before God. Thus these times became known as the hour of prayer. Prayer at these times continued even when sacrifices were not possible.

In addition to the morning and afternoon prayers, ancient Jews also developed a custom of praying in the evening as well. While this does not correspond to a sacrifice, it relates to the sacrificial leftovers that smoldered on the altar all night. The nighttime prayer is inspired by the words of Psalm 134:

> Come, bless the LORD, all you servants of the LORD, who stand by night in the house of the LORD! Lift up your hands to the holy place and bless the LORD! (Psalm 134:1-2)

One can pray at any time of the day. These particular times each day, however, are when Jewish people join for prayer.

BIBLICAL TIMES OF PRAYER

The Scriptures refer to these times of prayer. King David wrote, "Evening and morning and at noon I utter my complaint and moan, and he hears my voice" (Psalm 55:17).

The Prophet Daniel lived in Babylon during a time when the Jewish people could not offer sacrifices. When King Darius signed a decree prohibiting prayer to anyone but himself, Daniel was not fazed. "When Daniel knew that the document had been signed, he went to his house where he had windows in his upper chamber open toward Jerusalem. He got down on his knees three times a day and prayed and gave thanks before his God, as he had done previously" (Daniel 6:10).

Luke describes a typical morning in the Temple: "The whole multitude of the people were praying outside at the hour of incense" (Luke 1:10). This incense went up in smoke together with the morning burnt offering at sunrise.

Jesus himself rose early to pray: "Rising very early in the morning, while it was still dark, he departed and went out to a desolate place, and there he prayed" (Mark 1:35). Jewish writings describe an ancient custom of meditating for an hour before praying at sunrise, which may correspond to this practice of Jesus.

The book of Acts depicts the disciples on their way to the Temple for the afternoon prayers: "Peter and John were going up to the temple at the hour of prayer, the ninth hour" (Acts 3:1). The "ninth hour" is a conventional, ancient Jewish way to express the time of day.

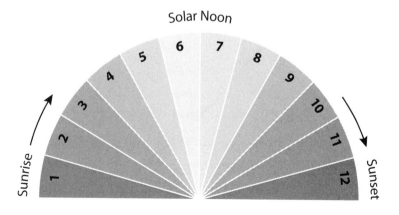

To calculate hours in the Jewish system of time, we divide the daylight period from sunrise to sunset into twelve equal portions. The ninth hour describes not an exact minute but a slice of the day in mid-afternoon.

This afternoon hour of prayer was the same time of day at which Cornelius offered his prayer (Acts 10:30).

THE ADDITIONAL PRAYER

Peter took in a deep breath of fresh sea air as he climbed the stone stairs. It was only the tanner's house, not the tannery, and yet the putrid smell inside squelched his appetite. There on the housetop the midday sun cast a small, crisp shadow beneath his feet.

"O Lord, open my lips, and my mouth will declare your praise" (Psalm 51:15), Peter whispered as he began his new moon prayer.

❖ ❖ ❖

Numbers 28 teaches about the daily burnt offering, then continues by describing other related time-based offerings. These offerings did not occur every day but only on the weekly Sabbath, monthly new moons, and yearly festivals. The priests presented these offerings in addition to the twice-daily sacrifice.

In keeping with the pattern, this additional sacrifice on holy days inspires an additional opportunity for prayer. In synagogues today congregations meet for morning prayers every day of the week. On the Sabbath, new moons, and festivals, an extra prayer accounts for this additional sacrifice.

When the Temple stood, the priests typically presented this sacrifice during the sixth hour of the day. In theory, however, the priests could bring this additional offering any time after the morning sacrifice.

In the absence of sacrifices today, it is no longer customary to wait until the sixth hour for this prayer. Instead, people usually recite it shortly after the morning prayer. But when the Temple stood, it would have been ideal to synchronize one's prayer with the actual offering:

> The next day, as they were on their journey and approaching the city, Peter went up on the housetop about the sixth hour to pray. (Acts 10:9)

This is why Peter went up on the rooftop to pray at the sixth hour—too late for the morning prayer and too early for the afternoon. We might even presume that Peter's vision occurred specifically on the new moon. Had it been a Sabbath or a festival day, we would see some detail to this effect, and the story would likely have taken place in the synagogue. The day of the new moon, on the other hand, is not much different from a typical day of the week, apart from the additional prayer.

THE MESSIAH'S SACRIFICE

The sacrifices of the Temple beautifully prefigure the suffering and death of the Messiah. This is true not only regarding the Passover lamb the ancient Jews roasted and ate at their Passover meals. All the many sacrifices and offerings connect in some way to the atoning suffering and death of Messiah.

For example, the sacrifices involve the shedding of blood, and they also have a certain ability to purify and draw one near to God. Beyond this, there is a remarkable correspondence even in their timing:

It was the third hour when they crucified him. (Mark 15:25)

Jesus was placed on the cross at the third hour. The third hour corresponds to the conclusion of the morning sacrificial service. It was at this time of day when, fifty days later, the disciples gathered on the Festival of Shavu'ot, also known as Pentecost (Acts 2:15).

When the sixth hour had come, there was darkness over the whole land until the ninth hour. (Mark 15:33)

Darkness covered the land at the sixth hour. The sixth hour corresponds to the time of the additional festival offering. Jesus died at the time of Passover and the Festival of Unleavened Bread. As with all the festivals, an additional offering was prescribed for this time (Numbers 28:16–25).

At the ninth hour Jesus cried with a loud voice, "*Eloi, Eloi, lema sabachthani?*" which means, "My God, my God, why have you forsaken me?" (Mark 15:34)

Jesus died at the ninth hour of the day. His death corresponds to the daily afternoon offering, the final sacrifice of each day. After this offering, the doors of the Sanctuary were closed.

Even the evening prayer reflects Jesus' suffering in some way. It was at night that he was arrested, accused, and beaten.

This correspondence suggests that by praying at the times of sacrifice, we are in a sense memorializing the Messiah and his suffering on our behalf.

THREE TIMES A DAY

The Jewish practice of daily prayer carried forth into Christian practice in later centuries. The *Didache* is a manual of practice for Gentile followers of Jesus, and it dates back to the first century.

This document instructed Gentile disciples of Jesus to pray the Lord's Prayer three times each day—a simple way to involve new Gentile followers of the Messiah in the rhythm of Jewish worship.

Over time this practice evolved into the canonical hours still practiced by Catholic and Orthodox churches. Yet when Paul spoke of these, he was referring to the prerogatives of the Jewish people:

> They are Israelites, and to them belong the adoption, the glory, the covenants, the giving of the law, the worship [literally: "service"], and the promises. (Romans 9:4)

That is not to say that Gentiles cannot participate in this pattern of worship as well. It is just that when they do, they are participating in something Jewish. They are joining in, reverberating with, and responding to the rhythm and pace set by the Jewish people.

As the earth spins on its axis, these daily appointed times flow across its surface like rippling waves. As they sweep over each town and city, Jewish people assemble in synagogues and enthrone the name of God in unison. These waves have been circling the earth continually for thousands of years.

When disciples of Jesus join in with this chorus of worship, we have the opportunity to infuse it with the power of the name of the Messiah.

Turning toward Jerusalem

The Geographical Center of God's Interaction with His World

Hannah's quivering hands stroked the infant's head; Simeon's arms cradled the baby Yeshua. Simeon exclaimed, "My eyes have seen your salvation [yeshu'ah] that you have prepared in the presence of all peoples, a light for revelation to the Gentiles, and for glory to your people Israel" (Luke 2:30–32). Hannah overflowed with the news to everyone around her that this child was the hope of the redemption of Jerusalem.

This was Jesus' first visit to Jerusalem but certainly not his last. As observant Jews, Mary and Joseph made the pilgrimage to Jerusalem year after year (Luke 2:41). Although Jesus grew up in the Galilean town of Nazareth, Jerusalem was his spiritual home.

❖   ❖   ❖

Jews all over the world turn to face Jerusalem for prayer. This custom has a strong biblical basis and goes back to ancient times.

Jerusalem is centered on Mount Moriah, where Isaac was prepared as a sacrifice. Its Hebrew name, *Yerushalayim*, is a combination of the names that Abraham and Melchizedek gave it: Abraham called it *Adonai Yireh* ("the LORD will see"), and Melchizedek called it *shalem* ("whole," "peaceful").

In the time of Moses, God anticipated Jerusalem's sacred role as his dwelling place. He commanded, "You shall seek the place that the LORD your God will choose out of all your tribes to put his name and make his habitation there" (Deuteronomy 12:5).

Ever since King David established Jerusalem as the united capital of the tribes of Israel and made it the home of the ark of the covenant, Jerusalem has been the focal point of Jewish spiritual life on earth.

Despite his awareness that our physical universe cannot contain its Creator, King Solomon knew that this city would somehow be a place where man and God could meet. Solomon perceived Jerusalem not only as a pilgrimage site but as a physical focal point for prayer. In his prayer at the dedication of the Temple, he asked that God would hear the prayers made toward the Temple, the city, and the land of Israel (1 Kings 8:23–61).

Furthermore, this holy site was not just the Jewish capital but the spiritual center of the entire world. Solomon asked God to hear the prayers of foreigners who prayed toward Jerusalem (1 Kings 8:41). Even when Jews were driven away from the land of Israel, Solomon indicated that they would turn and face the land of Israel (1 Kings 8:48).

Though the Temple lay in ruins and Daniel was far away in Babylon,

> He went to his house where he had windows in his upper chamber open toward Jerusalem. He got down on his knees three times a day and prayed and gave thanks before his God, as he had done previously. (Daniel 6:10)

Can a geographical place on earth be a dwelling place for an infinite God? Apparently in some sense it can.

No wonder why Jesus stayed behind in his "Father's house" when the others had turned back to Nazareth, why Mary and Joseph made the pilgrimage to Jerusalem every year, why Simeon waited there, and why Hannah never left the Temple courts. It explains why Jesus wept over Jerusalem as he prophetically beheld its destruction (Matthew 23:37–39; Luke 13:34–35).

All these were aware that even though God transcends the universe and the whole earth is full of his glory, Jerusalem is special. It is a place where one can hear the heartbeat of God.

Jerusalem's Future

The eleven disciples stood breathless with mouths open, staring into the sky. Their feet remained firmly planted in their sandals atop the Mount of Olives, but where the Messiah had just been standing were now only empty footprints. Not only had Jesus soared into the sky from Jerusalem's Mount of Olives, but Zechariah 14:4 confirmed that this was where he would return "in the same way as [they] saw him go into heaven" (Acts 1:11).

❖ ❖ ❖

Jerusalem by no means lost its significance after the death, burial, resurrection, and ascension of Jesus took place there. It remains the starting place and focal point for God's activities on earth, especially as we near the end times.

The prophets depict for us a beautiful future when the Messiah returns. He will establish the kingdom of heaven on earth, which will span the entire world; Jerusalem will be the capital, where Jesus will establish his throne. This message of the kingdom of God was at the core of the gospel that Jesus taught, and that is why he proclaimed his message so strongly in Jerusalem.

The list of end-times prophecies involving Jerusalem is far too extensive to include here, but we will mention a few.

Often the prophets endearingly referred to Jerusalem by the name "Zion," after one of the city's great hills.

In the Messianic Kingdom, living water will flow out from Jerusalem (Zechariah 14:8). The city will be rebuilt, never to be destroyed (Zechariah 14:11).

Ultimately Jerusalem will be the site of the annual pilgrimage for all nations:

> Then everyone who survives of all the nations that have come against Jerusalem shall go up year after year to worship the King, the LORD of hosts, and to keep the Feast of Booths. (Zechariah 14:16)

Isaiah envisioned Jerusalem as the hub of knowledge and justice in the messianic future:

> It shall come to pass in the latter days that the mountain of the house of the LORD shall be established as the highest of the mountains, and shall be lifted up above the hills; and all the nations shall flow to it, and many peoples shall come, and say: "Come, let us go up to the mountain of the LORD, to the house of the God of Jacob, that he may teach us his ways and that we may walk in his paths." For out of Zion shall go forth the law, and the word of the LORD from Jerusalem. (Isaiah 2:2–3)

The Prophet Joel described Jerusalem as the dwelling place of God:

> The LORD roars from Zion, and utters his voice from Jerusalem, and the heavens and the earth quake. But

the LORD is a refuge to his people, a stronghold to the
people of Israel. So you shall know that I am the LORD
your God, who dwells in Zion, my holy mountain. And
Jerusalem shall be holy, and strangers shall never again
pass through it. (Joel 3:16–17)

Considering these prophecies, it is no surprise that in the book
of Revelation, God promises to send down a New Jerusalem from
heaven. This promise shows that Jerusalem is and always will be
at the center of God's interaction with the world.

When we turn to face Jerusalem in prayer, we envision it not as
it is but as it will be when Jesus returns. Doing so places our prayers
in the context of the Messianic Kingdom and expresses our hope
in the soon-coming Messiah. It shows that we await God's solution
to all our problems: the redemption of Jerusalem.

Jerusalem in the Early Church

*About 120 Jewish men and women, followers of Jesus of
Nazareth, gathered together in Solomon's Colonnade under
the shade of its cedar beams. They assembled for prayer in
the Temple courts alongside Jews from all over the world in
honor of the biblical festival called Shavu'ot, or Pentecost.*

*In obedience to Jesus' command, these disciples had
remained in Jerusalem after the Lord's ascension. It was
there in the city that they received the gift of the Holy Spirit.
In Jerusalem they were transformed from a small band of
disciples into a true* ekklesia *("assembly").*

Just before his ascension, Jesus told his followers that they would
be his witnesses in Jerusalem, in all Judea and Samaria, and to the

ends of the earth (Acts 1:8). Notice how Jesus himself envisioned the world with Jerusalem at its center.

Jerusalem is mentioned no less than fifty-eight times in the book of Acts alone. The followers of Jesus met regularly in Solomon's Portico, an area within the Temple courts. And even as the message spread across the region, Jerusalem remained the home base of the apostles. Paul collected donations from other communities of believers and brought them to the apostolic community in the holy city.

Like other Jews, first-century followers of Messiah faced Jerusalem when they prayed. The city represented for them the hope of redemption and the second coming of Jesus.

As the church began to distance herself from her Jewish roots, reverence for Jerusalem was lost. Instead of facing Jerusalem in prayer, Christians began to adopt the more universal custom of simply facing east regardless of location. This is the custom among Orthodox Christians to this day.

But today more and more Christians recognize Jerusalem as the "apple of God's eye," knowing that this will be the place of Messiah's glorious return. It makes sense for non-Jewish believers to stand in solidarity with the Jewish people in our day and return to the ancient practice.

SPIRITUAL JERUSALEM

Why turn to face a physical place? Didn't Jesus say to the Samaritan woman that true worshipers will worship the Father in spirit and in truth (John 4:23)? Isn't the present Jerusalem "in slavery," while the Jerusalem above is "our mother" (Galatians 4:25–26)? Doesn't the body of Messiah now constitute the Temple and dwelling place for God by the Spirit (Ephesians 2:19–22)?

In speaking to the Samaritan woman, Jesus confirmed that the Jewish people possessed the true revelation of God. He told her,

"You worship what you do not know; we worship what we know, for salvation is from the Jews" (John 4:22). But Jesus was aware that only one generation later the Romans would ransack the Temple and tear it down to its foundation. Despite the Temple's holy, chosen status and glorious future, it would not always be physically possible to pray there. Nevertheless, we worship in spirit, turning our hearts toward Jerusalem and anticipating God's future plans. (Thank God, in our time Jerusalem is inhabited by Jews once more, and people once again worship there every day!)

In Galatians Paul contrasts the "present Jerusalem" with the "Jerusalem above." But this is not a new idea that originated with Paul. The ancient rabbis also knew and talked about the "Jerusalem above." This idea in no way minimizes the importance of physical Jerusalem—actually, it emphasizes it. After all, how many cities have a heavenly version? It just shows that our Jerusalem on earth is a physical representative of a tremendous spiritual reality.

Similarly, the concept of a spiritual temple did not originate with Christianity. For example, the ancient rabbis looked closely at the verse, "Let them make me a sanctuary, that I may dwell in their midst" (Exodus 25:8). In Hebrew this verse can also be understood as, "They will make me a sanctuary, but I will dwell within them." In other words, God's faithful people have always constituted a dwelling place for his Spirit.

This interpretation illustrates an important concept in the Jewish frame of mind: physical and spiritual realities can exist simultaneously. The heavenly Tabernacle already existed before God commanded Moses to build one on earth; the heavenly Tabernacle was the "pattern" God showed him on the mountain (Exodus 25:9). One does not negate or obviate the other.

Turning the Heart

If a person doesn't know which way Jerusalem is, or if turning toward the city is just not practical in someone's time and place, not to worry. We do not pray to Jerusalem; we pray to our Father in heaven. We should direct our hearts toward him.

There is nothing magical about facing a certain direction in prayer. God can hear our prayers even if we speak into a hole in the ground! It certainly has no bearing on our salvation.

Prayer is communication. Communication takes place not only through the words we speak but also through our body language. Think of what it conveys when a person faces away from us while speaking or when someone's eyes are darting around the room. What would that kind of distraction look like in prayer?

The author of Hebrews invokes Zion and Jerusalem as symbolic of the new covenant enacted through our Messiah:

> You have come to Mount Zion and to the city of the living God, the heavenly Jerusalem, and to innumerable angels in festal gathering, and to the assembly of the firstborn who are enrolled in heaven, and to God, the judge of all, and to the spirits of the righteous made perfect, and to Jesus, the mediator of a new covenant, and to the sprinkled blood that speaks a better word than the blood of Abel. (Hebrews 12:22–24)

By turning to face Jerusalem, we express to God our desire to step into line with his plans and purposes in this world. We show that he has our full attention. We communicate that we are eager to see Messiah return.

When Christians turn their hearts and faces toward the holy city, anticipating its redemption and transformation through Messiah, they stand in unity with their Jewish brothers and sisters all across the world. They unite with countless generations of Jewish people going back to the earliest followers of Jesus.

In Yeshua's Name

How the Righteousness of Jesus Grants Us Access to God

In a small village in a great kingdom was a simple innkeeper. He wanted to make a request before the king, but how could he do so? One day a nobleman was passing through the village and stayed in the inn. The innkeeper thought, "If I treat this nobleman well, perhaps he can take my request to the king." So he gave the nobleman the best treatment he could offer.

"Thank you for your splendid service," the nobleman said.

The innkeeper seized his opportunity. "Would you bring a request of mine to the king?"

"I will do better than that," the nobleman insisted. He brought the innkeeper into his carriage, dressed him in fine clothes, and took him to the king's palace to make the request himself.

❖ ❖ ❖

Jesus taught us to address our prayers to the Father. He said, "Pray then like this: 'Our Father in heaven ...'" (Matthew 6:9). Yet we have a problem. Who are we to speak before the King of the universe? How does a mortal and sinful man dare to make requests before God?

As disciples of Jesus, we need not worry. We can come confidently before God because, according to the New Testament, Jesus is our mediator in prayer.

There are two possible kinds of mediator. One kind, which we might refer to as an intermediary, is a go-between. When such an intermediary is present, the two parties communicating remain separate and speak only through the third party. In contrast, a true mediator is one who brings two parties together, reconciling them and eliminating the distance and barriers between them.

By these definitions Jesus is a true mediator, not an intermediary. His righteous life, sacrificial death, and post-resurrection intercession on our behalf pave the way for us to have direct access to God our Father with no barriers and no person in our way.

First John 2:1 calls Jesus our "advocate." The ancient rabbis used this word to explain a pattern they noticed in the book of Leviticus: one must always bring a sin offering first before a burnt offering. Why would this be? Why couldn't a person offer a burnt offering alone?

The rabbis explained it by comparing it to a person who wishes to bring a gift to the king but does not have the king's favor. According to the rabbis, a sin offering is like an advocate who enters the king's palace first to gain his favor on behalf of the person. Once the advocate has gained the king's favor, the person may bring his gift. The advocate uses his own standing and merit to provide the petitioner direct access to the king.

Likewise, a sin offering comes first because it provides reconciliation. It paves the way for the burnt offering, which is an expression of love.

Paul taught in a similar way about Jesus when he said, "For our sake he made him to be sin who knew no sin, so that in him we might become the righteousness of God" (2 Corinthians 5:21).

Did Jesus become sin? How does this even make sense? By reading this verse with the mindset of the Hebrew language, it becomes clearer. The Hebrew word for "sin" is also the word for "sin offering." Jesus was without sin, so he became a sin offering on our behalf. Like a sin offering, he reconciles us to God through his own merit and by acting as our advocate.

REPRESENTATIVES OF MESSIAH

What does it mean to ask the Father "in Jesus' name?" Many people treat this as a formula for prayer that we say just before signing off: "In Jesus' name, amen." There is nothing wrong with saying this, but Jewish wisdom provides access to the deeper meaning behind this concept.

The idiom "in the name of" in Hebrew means "as a representative of" or "on the authority of." If we ask God for something in Jesus' name, we are asking the Father to respond to us because of our association with Jesus. In a way, we are merely the messenger; the request actually belongs to him. When we ask in Jesus' name, it is not Jesus who represents us before God; it is we who represent Jesus:

> In that day you will ask in my name, and I do not say to you that I will ask the Father on your behalf; for the Father himself loves you, because you have loved me and have believed that I came from God. (John 16:26–27)

It is a little bit like a person who receives a company credit card. He makes purchases on behalf of the company because he has been delegated the authority to do so. The payment, as large as it may be, can be made because it is drawn on the company credit card. In the same way, as disciples of Jesus, we have the privilege of drawing on Jesus' credit as we make our needs known to God.

This example implies two things. First, God accepts the petitions on our lips due to the merit and virtue of Yeshua—not our own. Second, asking in Jesus' name is not a license to name and claim whatever we like. Instead, we have license to ask only for things that pertain to our capacity as Jesus' agents in the world, and whatever we do receive in his name ultimately belongs to him and not to us.

Praying in his merit and as his representative is what it means to pray in Jesus' name. It does not require saying the words "in Jesus' name" as a formula or that every prayer must end with "in Jesus' name, amen." On the other hand, it is quite common in Judaism to include legal formalities when praying, and thus it is appropriate to mention Jesus and request that God answer our prayers on his behalf.

THE TZADDIK

Surely God was accessible and answered prayers before Jesus came. This raises questions about how Jesus benefits us as a mediator and why it is necessary for us to ask for things in his name.

Psalm 145:18–19 promises,

> The LORD is near to all who call on him, to all who call on him in truth. He fulfills the desire of those who fear him; he also hears their cry and saves them.

Furthermore, we can see examples of individuals who called upon God and were answered. Elijah is just such an example: his prayers stopped and started the rain. Was Jesus his mediator?

These examples notwithstanding, we know from experience and history that scriptures such as these describe an ideal principle rather than an inviolable law of the cosmos. It often happens that individuals pray but do not receive the answer they desire.

Jewish literature contains stories about how in times of distress, the sages of Israel sought out individuals whose prayers God frequently answered:

> Once it happened that the son of Rabban Gamliel became sick. He sent two scholars to Rabbi Chanina ben Dosa to pray for mercy on his behalf. When he saw them, he went to the upper room and prayed for mercy on his behalf. When he came back down, he told them, "Go; the fever has left him." They asked him, "How would you know that? Are you a prophet?" He told them, "I am not a prophet, nor am I the son of a prophet, but this is what I have learned: If my prayer is smooth in my mouth, I know that it is accepted, but if not, I know that it is denied." They sat down and took note of the exact moment when this happened. When they returned to Rabban Gamliel, he told them, "I swear that you have not added or subtracted a single moment! That was the very time that the fever left him and he asked us for water to drink."

This story is only one of numerous accounts of healings and miracles performed by Rabbi Chanina ben Dosa and a few other individuals like him. A student of the Gospels cannot help but notice the similarity these stories bear to events that took place during Jesus' ministry.

Passages like this raise a few questions. Why did Rabban Gamliel have to send scholars to Rabbi Chanina ben Dosa? Couldn't Rabban Gamliel have prayed on his own? Couldn't the two scholars have prayed and received an answer for themselves?

The scholars recognized that there was something unique about Rabbi Chanina. His prayers were frequently answered because he was an exceptionally righteous individual. Though he was human like everyone else, Rabbi Chanina had merit and standing before

God that most people did not. The same goes for individuals in the Bible like Elijah.

The Hebrew word for a righteous person is *tzaddik*. Can a person be righteous?

Surely we all fall short and rely on God for mercy and salvation. Yet the Scriptures provide several examples of people who are righteous and gain God's favor. Noah is a good example:

> Noah was a righteous man, blameless in his generation. Noah walked with God. (Genesis 6:9)

Noah may not have been perfect, but the Bible calls him a tzaddik, a righteous man, and he found favor in God's eyes (Genesis 6:8). Thus, it was through Noah that God saved the world.

For this reason people naturally turn to righteous individuals for prayer. Moses was able to gain forgiveness for the Israelites who had sinned because he found favor with God (Exodus 33:17). The people turned to the Prophet Jeremiah to ask for prayer after Ishmael killed Gedaliah (Jeremiah 42:1–4). The people turned to Samuel to ask him to pray for them for the sin of asking for a king (1 Samuel 12:19).

The New Testament attests to this concept. James teaches us,

> Confess your sins to one another and pray for one another, that you may be healed. The prayer of a righteous person [i.e., a tzaddik] has great power as it is working. Elijah was a man with a nature like ours, and he prayed fervently that it might not rain, and for three years and six months it did not rain on the earth. Then he prayed again, and heaven gave rain, and the earth bore its fruit. (James 5:16–18)

This instruction from James accords well with other Jewish teachings on this topic. The ancient rabbis taught that one who is sick should seek the prayers of the elders, based on Proverbs

16:14: "A king's wrath is a messenger of death, and a wise man will appease it."

Centuries later, many Jews still embrace this idea. Paul Philip Levertoff was a Jewish believer in Jesus who was raised in a prestigious Chasidic Jewish family. Here is how he explained the belief among Chasidic Jews:

> The tzaddik is the pet or favorite of heaven, the instrument through which God sends his grace into the world. Through his communion with God, he is the connection between God and creation, and as such, he is the bearer and mediator of blessing and grace. The love that man has for the tzaddik is therefore the means through which God's grace is won. The duty of every Chasid is this: that he loves the tzaddik and listens to his word.

Understood this way, Jesus is the ultimate tzaddik. He has earned merit and favor before God that not even Elijah or Rabbi Chanina achieved. It is not as though God will not hear our prayers directly, but rather, does he have a good reason to answer them? By clinging to Jesus—that is, identifying with him, following him, and trusting in him—we benefit from his merit, and God answers our prayers on his account.

However, it bears repeating that we do not bring our requests to Jesus so that he may in turn relay them to our heavenly Father, as the scholars did with Rabbi Chanina. Rather, his merit benefits us directly, because when we pray to God, we do so as disciples of Jesus.

Although as individuals we are faulty and undeserving, God accords us the honor due to a tzaddik because we stand before him in the capacity of Jesus' official representatives. And just as God shows such favor to us, we, too, should treat fellow disciples as bearing the merit of Jesus, even if they do not deserve it in and of themselves.

Seeking the Kingdom

The Most Important
Prayer in Jewish Life

The king's fury burned against his son for his defiance. He sent his son out of the palace empty-handed.

Penniless, the exiled prince wandered from village to village begging for bread. Finally, a local villager extended a hand and offered him employment as a servant. The king's son worked hard for several years in exchange for meals and boarding. Over time, however, his master reduced his rations while demanding harder and harder work.

Years later the king wondered about the welfare of his son, so he set out to the villages to find him. Wherever he went, crowds came to him to ask him to settle their grievances. When the king came to his village, the exiled prince also stood in line with his own request.

When the prince finally stood before the king, his father's face lit up. "What is your request?" he asked.

"Please, your highness, tell my master to give me bread to eat and not to treat me so harshly," the prince asked.

The king was astonished. "Have you forgotten who you are? Why are you asking for a stale piece of bread? Ask to be restored to your home in the palace!"

❖ ❖ ❖

Often when we pray, we focus on our acute problems. Expenses, relationships, ailments, and other day-to-day problems occupy our minds. It is good to pray about those things, but are we seeking treatment for the symptoms while neglecting the disease?

Jesus taught,

> Do not be anxious, saying, "What shall we eat?" or "What shall we drink?" or "What shall we wear?" For the Gentiles seek after all these things, and your heavenly Father knows that you need them all. But seek first the kingdom of God and his righteousness, and all these things will be added to you. (Matthew 6:31–33)

At the core of Jesus' message is the prophetic hope of redemption. The history of Israel has been tumultuous and difficult, but the prophets foretold a time of peace and prosperity. When that time comes, Israel will dwell in security on her own land. The Messiah will be seated on the throne of David in Jerusalem, dispensing justice and godly wisdom to the whole earth. All nations will recognize the God of Israel as the only true God and King of the whole universe. The ancient Jewish sages referred to this ideal future as "the days of Messiah." Jesus called it "the kingdom of heaven."

Such a hope is still clear in the pages of the Bible and the teachings of Jesus, and the Jewish community today still holds it dear.

This kingdom is not merely something that happens beyond our control. We strive for it. We seek to enter it. We pray for this kingdom to come. Scripture even teaches that by our conduct we should be "hastening the coming of the day of God" (2 Peter 3:12).

Because of this, Jewish prayer tends to be grand in its aspirations. Instead of merely praying for healing for a specific ailment, why not pray for the complete spiritual and physical healing that will come to all in the Messianic Kingdom? Instead of asking only for a particular financial need, why not ask for the overwhelming abundance of the coming Messianic Era?

Audience with the King

In the Western world today, we can hardly comprehend the notion of a king. We perceive our governmental leaders as people much like ourselves. Checks and balances limit their authority and guarantee that they submit to the rule of law. Standing in the presence of our national leaders, the average person may feel a bit star-struck, but that is all.

This sense of human equality is a positive development of our society. However, in the process of gaining it, we have lost the experience of overwhelming awe, reverence, and fear in the presence of majesty. We tend to gravitate to notions of God as our loving Father and companion—both of which he surely is. But our generation tends to be uncomfortable envisioning him as the supreme power who deserves and demands complete submission and servitude.

In the Jewish mind, prayer is audience with the King of the universe. When Jews pray, they enter his palace and stand before his throne. Though this is spiritual, it is a reality. As such, Jewish custom is to prepare oneself mentally, spiritually, and physically for prayer. Just as one would not dare insult a mortal king by appearing before him in dirty clothes or in a poor state of mind, so observant Jews clean up and focus their minds for prayer.

Prayer services in the synagogue reflect a spiritual journey into the heavenly Temple. The preliminary prayers represent the outer courts. With each prayer, one moves closer and closer into the most sacred chambers. Corresponding to the holy of holies, an ancient prayer called the *Amidah* is the high point of every synagogue service.

Most Jewish prayers are to be recited aloud in a clear voice. The *Amidah*, however, is uttered in a mere whisper. This custom reflects the concept that God is intimately close and attentive at the holy moment of its pronouncement.

The Hebrew word *amidah* means "standing." The prayer gets its name from the custom of standing to recite it, just as we envision ourselves standing before the throne of God. Jesus referred to this posture in prayer when he said, "Whenever you stand praying, forgive, if you have anything against anyone, so that your Father also who is in heaven may forgive you your trespasses" (Mark 11:25).

This prayer existed in some form well before the coming of Jesus. He and his disciples would have been intimately familiar with it. Early church writings show that Christians as late as the fourth century CE were still reciting prayers based on the *Amidah*.

The *Amidah* prayer is a series of nineteen blessings. The first three blessings are expressions of praise. The last three are expressions of thanks. The thirteen in the middle are petitions. Each of these petitions relates in some sense to the glorious return of Messiah and the establishment of his kingdom on earth.

The Sabbath and Jewish festivals are spiritual glimpses of the coming Messianic Kingdom—a "shadow of the things to come" (Colossians 2:17). Accordingly, on those days the thirteen petitions are replaced by a single blessing thanking God for the holiness of the day, leaving a total of seven blessings.

Here are the topics covered in this prayer:

1. PROMISES AND COVENANTS

We praise God for his promises and the covenants that he made with Abraham, Isaac, and Jacob. It is on the basis of these covenant promises that God has sustained, blessed, and protected the Jewish people. Among these promises, God swore to send the Messiah to redeem his people and the entire world.

2. MIRACLES AND RESURRECTION

We acknowledge that God's power transcends nature. It is in God's character to restore, heal, and revive. This blessing expresses faith that he takes care of his creatures by upholding those who fall, healing the sick, and releasing people from bondage. He even brings the dead back to life!

3. THE HOLINESS OF GOD'S NAME

We describe and take part in the heavenly worship of the angels. As Isaiah saw in his vision and John in his Revelation, the angels surround God's throne continually, crying, "Holy, holy, holy!" In this prayer we ask God to sanctify his name on earth just as it is sanctified in heaven.

4. KNOWLEDGE

We ask God that he give us all greater wisdom, discernment, and knowledge. In Jewish thought knowledge implies an intimate, firsthand experience. Our goal in life is to know God and be in relationship with him. When the Messiah returns, the whole world will know God (Isaiah 11:9; Jeremiah 31:34).

5. REPENTANCE

We ask God to open our hearts and the hearts of everyone to repent. This acknowledges that even our ability to turn from sin is a gift from God.

6. FORGIVENESS

We admit that as God's people, we have fallen short. We ask for his forgiveness, that he relinquish his anger toward us. We also ask for his pardon, that he wipe away any debt we owe him on account of our sins. This is similar to what Jesus taught us to pray: "Forgive us our debts, as we also have forgiven our debtors" (Matthew 6:12).

7. REDEMPTION

The world is full of suffering. Slavery and captivity still exist in many forms. We ask God to fight on behalf of victimized and exploited people, freeing them from bondage. Just as Jesus cared for the downtrodden in his first coming, when he returns, he will grant freedom and victory to all those who are suffering.

8. HEALING

We know that true healing comes from God, who restores us both physically and spiritually. We ask him to heal everyone of all our ailments. When the Messiah came to Israel, he healed the sick, blind, and crippled as well as those with mental illness, spiritual oppression, and broken hearts. The same healing will characterize the entire world when he comes again.

9. ABUNDANT HARVEST

We ask that this would be a year of abundant crops and food, that rain will fall where it is needed. By extension, we can ask that abundance and blessing will replace poverty and need in all areas of life. Just as Jesus multiplied food to feed thousands, when he comes again, hunger will no longer plague the world.

10. INGATHERING

Jesus taught that at his coming "he will send out his angels with a loud trumpet call, and they will gather his elect from the four winds, from one end of heaven to the other" (Matthew 24:31). In saying this he echoed the words of the prophets, who foretold the gathering of the scattered Jewish people into the land of Israel.

We have begun to see just such an ingathering with the establishment of the modern State of Israel and the waves of Jewish immigrants. We ask that the great shofar (ram's horn) would sound and all Jewish people would be brought back to the promised land.

11. JUSTICE

Corruption, greed, and a distorted sense of right and wrong dominate this world. We ask God to restore this world to true justice and that God's rule would prevail in compassion and fairness. We ask him to restore honest judges. Jesus said that his disciples would "sit on thrones judging the twelve tribes of Israel" (Luke 22:30). We long for the day when this takes place.

12. VICTORY OVER EVIL

In every generation there are those who attempt to destroy the Jewish people and oppose the kingdom of God in this world. While we share God's desire that sinners turn to him in repentance, we also ask that the evil forces that oppose God would be vanquished and brought to an end.

13. THE REWARD OF THE RIGHTEOUS

In this world those who do what is good rarely receive their reward. We know that they will indeed receive their treasures stored up in heaven when the kingdom of God comes. We ask that God would have compassion on the faithful and let us see that day soon.

14. The restoration of Jerusalem

God promised through the prophets that Jerusalem would be rebuilt and restored to glory, never to be destroyed again. We catch a glimpse of the ultimate fulfillment of this in Revelation 21 as the New Jerusalem descends from heaven adorned like a bride. In the meantime, we pray for the peace and well-being of Jerusalem, longing for the day when it is restored.

15. The Davidic kingdom

In the most explicitly messianic prayer of all, we ask God to restore the kingdom, setting the Branch of David upon his throne. We express to God that we long for and anticipate his salvation.

16. Acceptance

We ask for compassion and favor. We desire that God not be like the unrighteous judge who was bothered by the obnoxious voice of the claimant but that our voice would move him to true compassion. Just as God "heard our voice" at the time of the exodus from Egypt (Deuteronomy 26:7), we ask him to take pity on us today.

17. Worship

We ask for God's Sanctuary to be established on earth and that the sacrificial worship of the Jewish people be accepted as it once was. This prayer echoes many of the words of the prophets regarding the Messianic Kingdom (for example, see Ezekiel 37:26; Malachi 3:3–4).

Although this seems a bit like a petition, it is an expression of thanks in that the purpose of these services is to give thanks to God.

18. GOD'S GOODNESS

We thank God for the good things he does for us constantly. Sometimes these are overt miracles and answers to desperate prayer. Other times they are seemingly small things that happen every day. All these are miracles for which God is entitled to our thanks.

19. PEACE

Finally, we thank God who fills our lives with true *shalom* (peace). We ask him to continue to grant us peace, goodness, blessing, grace, kindness, and compassion. *Shalom* is not the mere cessation of war; it is complete health, wholeness, and well-being. Disciples of Jesus know that this comes through him.

AN OUTLINE FOR PRAYER

In some cases Christians might feel as if they already possess the answers to the prayers above. This makes sense, because if one is a disciple of Jesus, then that one is a member of his kingdom even now. Nonetheless, by participating in these prayers, Christians are not just asking on their own behalf; they are interceding for the Jewish people and the entire world.

All the same, it is good to mention our personal needs along with related petitions. For example, it is customary during the prayer for healing to mention the names of specific people who need healing and to ask for their complete recovery.

Many scholars have noted similarities between the structure and content of the *Amidah* and the Lord's Prayer. They share several common themes.

Whether or not non-Jewish believers choose to follow an outline like this in their prayer lives, it is good to consider expanding one's vision. We are to pray not only for our immediate needs but to seek the coming kingdom of God.

THE BREAD OF TOMORROW

THE LORD'S PRAYER IN ITS JEWISH CONTEXT

The teacher and his disciples gathered for morning prayers in the study hall. After the service ended, one of the students eagerly asked, "Rabbi, how do you pray?"

Rabbi Eliezer stared off into the distance, and his body swayed as he tapped his memory. In a sing-song tone he uttered, "If your prayer becomes a rigid habit, it is no longer a true supplication."

His disciple furled his brow in confusion. "How should it not be a habit? Are we not to say the Prayer three times each day?"

Rabbi Eliezer smiled. "One's prayer should not be like mindlessly reading a letter. In my prayer I include something new each day. And at the end of the Prayer, I say,

Let it be your will, O LORD our God, that you let love, brotherhood, peace, and companionship take up residence in our lives. Let our boundaries expand with disciples. Let us successfully finish with a future and hope, and make a place for us in the Garden of Eden. Affirm us with a good friend and a good inclination in your world. Let us rise each morning and find that the yearning in our heart is to fear your name. Let our spiritual needs come before you for the good.

❖ ❖ ❖

To one who is familiar with the language of Jewish prayer, there is no denying that the *Our Father*, otherwise known as the Lord's Prayer, is woven of Jewish fabric. Many of the rabbis of the first and second centuries, such as Rabbi Eliezer, appended a personal touch to the end of the *Amidah*, which they taught their disciples. Often these prayers use similar wording to what we find in the Gospels.

I once watched an online video of a man who, though teaching in English, spoke Hebrew as his first language, so he had a thick accent and limited vocabulary. I could understand him because I am familiar with the Israeli accent, but I decided to try reading the automatically generated subtitles. Because of his accent the site believed that he was speaking fluent Dutch. It then took the initiative to translate that into English for me. The result, of course, was gibberish.

The same thing can happen with the words of Jesus. The language of the Lord's Prayer is Jewish in its essence. If we read it as a Jewish prayer, its true meaning shines out. But one who is not familiar with Jewish prayers, expressions, and ways of thinking may not realize what he is missing.

It should not surprise us that the Lord's Prayer contains the same style of language as other Jewish prayers of its time. After all, Jesus was a faithful and observant Jew, and he taught his disciples in the context of the Jewish faith and culture. Familiarity with other Jewish prayers will help us perceive and understand the meaning of this prayer.

At the same time, the prayer that Jesus taught is unique and powerful. While it contains the same building blocks as other Jewish prayers, it has a special message that pertains to us, Jesus' disciples. In particular, the Lord's Prayer places a strong focus on the kingdom of heaven.

Most Christians are familiar with the Lord's Prayer in the King James version or a derivative of it. Because it is such a common feature in Christian liturgy, it may be jarring to hear other interpretations. A person should not let this prevent him from hearing it with fresh ears.

Of course, Jesus did not speak English at all. In his daily life he spoke a hybrid Hebrew-Aramaic that was common among Jews in his day. When praying or telling a parable, he would have followed the common convention of switching to pure Hebrew. Jews have always considered Hebrew to be the holy language.

To help spread his message to a wider audience, Jesus' disciples interpreted his words and teachings in the Greek language. Their Greek interpretation is the text that we have today in the New Testament. However, even in Greek, the words of Jesus bear indications of their original languages and preserve Hebraic patterns of thought.

Our Father which Art in Heaven

The phrase "Our Father who is in heaven" is a common Jewish way to address God, found in many prayers and writings.

Addressing God as "Father" draws attention to his compassion. This idea is in keeping with the gentle words of Psalm 103, which comforts us by saying, "As a father shows compassion to his children, so the LORD shows compassion to those who fear him" (Psalm 103:13). We say "who is in heaven" simply to differentiate God from a human father.

Hallowed Be Thy Name

"Hallowed" means "sanctified" or "treated as holy." Another way to word this line is "Let your name be sanctified." It is not a declaration or expression of worship; it is a petition.

The *Kaddish*, a famous and ancient Jewish prayer, opens with a similar line: "Let God's name be magnified and sanctified in the world that he created as he willed."

The Prophet Ezekiel teaches,

> When they came to the nations, wherever they came, they profaned my holy name, in that people said of them, "These are the people of the LORD, and yet they had to go out of his land." (Ezekiel 36:20)

"Profaned" is the opposite of "sanctified." As long as God's people suffer in exile, it seems to the surrounding nations that God is unable or unwilling to fulfill his promises. When God acts on his promises and fulfills them, his name is sanctified:

> I will vindicate the holiness of my great name, which has been profaned among the nations, and which you have profaned among them. And the nations will know that I am the LORD, declares the Lord GOD, when through you I vindicate my holiness before their eyes. (Ezekiel 36:23)

What does it look like when God redeems his people and sanctifies his name?

- ❖ *There is a miraculous ingathering*: "I will take you from the nations ... and bring you into your own land" (Ezekiel 36:24).

- ❖ *There is a prophetic purification*: "I will sprinkle clean water on you" (Ezekiel 36:25).

- ❖ *There is a spiritual regeneration*: "I will give you a new heart, and a new spirit" (Ezekiel 36:26).

In other words, when Ezekiel spoke of God sanctifying his name, he was referring to the new covenant promises of the Messianic

Kingdom. Some of these things we have already begun to experience. Most of it, however, we will see when the Messiah returns.

This is also the meaning of Jesus' words. As long as God's redemptive promises remain unfulfilled, his name is profaned. By asking for God's name to be sanctified, we plead for divine intervention in this world and the realization of God's prophetic promises.

THY KINGDOM COME

Again, the Lord's Prayer bears similarity to the *Kaddish*, which asks, "May he inaugurate his kingdom." This kingdom refers to the Messianic Era when all humanity will know and accept the sovereignty of God.

Zechariah 14 describes the messianic future, saying, "The LORD will be king over all the earth" (Zechariah 14:9). Obadiah likewise says, "The kingdom shall be the LORD's" (Obadiah 21).

Do these verses imply that the LORD is not currently King? The ancient Jewish interpreters were careful to clarify that God is and always has been King but that his kingdom is not yet revealed on earth. In the Messianic Era, "every knee shall bow" (Isaiah 45:23; Romans 14:11; Philippians 2:10), which is why Jesus refers to the Messianic Era as "the kingdom of God."

THY WILL BE DONE

Likewise, "Let your will be done" is a plea for the Messianic Era. In our present age, God hides himself. He refrains from doling out reward and punishment. But in the future world, God's desires will be expressly carried out.

In Earth, as It Is in Heaven

This phrase connects to all three of the previous requests. In other words, we should interpret this as:

- Let your name be sanctified—in earth, as it is in heaven.
- Let your kingdom come—in earth, as it is in heaven.
- Let your will be done—in earth, as it is in heaven.

In heaven the angels who surround God's throne sanctify his name. In heaven the angels recognize him and revere him as King. In heaven the angels carry out his will perfectly and without hesitation. We desire to see these dynamics of heaven taking place here on earth. These things will happen at the second coming when we see Jesus "seated at the right hand of Power and coming on the clouds of heaven" (Matthew 26:64).

Thus, the first long sentence of the Lord's Prayer is a plea that the Messianic Era will arrive. This goes hand in hand with what Jesus taught us: "Seek first the kingdom." It makes perfect sense that he would tell us to pray in this way.

Give Us This Day Our Daily Bread

After focusing on the grand arrival of the Messianic Kingdom, it is strange to ask, "Give me something to eat." Is that what Jesus truly meant, or is there a deeper meaning?

The English phrase "daily bread" seems straightforward. However, many modern translations contain footnotes explaining that this phrase can also be translated "bread for tomorrow." How can it mean both?

The Greek text is not that clear. The Greek word typically translated as "daily" is *epiousion* (επιούσιον). But this is not the normal way to say "daily" in Greek. What's more, it is not even a valid Greek word. Even the early church fathers who natively spoke Greek acknowledged that the word was made up. It does not appear in *any other* Greek literature.

To understand what this strange word means, we must break it into its component parts. We know that the first part is a versatile prefix (*epi*), which can mean "over" or "after."

The second part is where opinions vary. In one view the second root word is *einai*, which means "being." The resulting interpretation is "over-being." This conclusion is the source of the "daily bread" interpretation as if to say "the bread for the time being."

However, this interpretation causes a grammatical problem in Greek. If this were the root word, the compound word should be *epousion*, not *epiousion*. (The first *iota* should disappear.)

Another possibility is that the second root word is *ienai*, which means "coming." The resulting interpretation is "coming-after." A similar word shows up in the Greek version of Proverbs and means "tomorrow." By this interpretation the verse means, "Give us today our 'tomorrowly' bread," that is, our bread of tomorrow.

The fourth-century theologian Jerome and several other church fathers occasionally referred to a document called the Gospel of the Hebrews. It was a collection of sayings and stories about Jesus used by his Jewish disciples, written in the Hebrew language. Unfortunately, this document is no longer extant. According to Jerome, this version used the Hebrew word for "tomorrow," not "daily."

In all, the evidence is quite strong that "tomorrow" is the correct reading. While scholars are aware of this, people are so accustomed to the interpretation in the King James that anything else would seem wrong to them.

It also raises the question, why would we ask for tomorrow's bread today? Jesus taught us not to be anxious about tomorrow. But the "bread of tomorrow" is not talking about regular food. As Jerome explained,

The Hebrew Gospel according to Matthew reads, "Give us today the bread of tomorrow," in other words, the bread that you will give us in your kingdom, give today.

So this "tomorrowly" bread is the bread of the Messianic Kingdom. The kingdom is frequently described in terms of a great banquet. Someone reclining at a meal with Jesus once reacted to his teachings by exclaiming, "Blessed is everyone who will eat bread in the kingdom of God!" (Luke 14:15). In the book of Revelation Jesus promises that "to the one who conquers [he] will give some of the hidden manna" (Revelation 2:17).

Thus, by asking for the bread of tomorrow to come to us today, we are asking for the substance of the Messianic Era to be present in our daily lives even as we strive in the current age. We also express the hope that today is the day when we will finally feast at the lavish banquet of the Messianic Kingdom.

FORGIVE US OUR DEBTS, AS WE FORGIVE OUR DEBTORS

When others wrong us, we often feel as if they owe us some kind of repayment or are liable for our suffering. In the same way, when we sin, we owe a debt to God. Yet this is not so much a prayer for personal forgiveness. As in many Jewish prayers, this phrase is spoken in the collective voice, speaking of the entire nation.

The choice of "debt" here as a reference to sin is significant. In the ancient world, when a person fell deeply into debt he could not repay, he became a slave. In Jewish terminology, freeing slaves by releasing them from their debts is "redemption":

> If your brother becomes poor and sells part of his property, then his nearest redeemer shall come and redeem what his brother has sold. (Leviticus 25:25)

God instructed through Moses that Jewish debtors were not to remain slaves forever. Every seven years there was to be a year of forgiving debts:

> At the end of every seven years you shall grant a release. And this is the manner of the release: every creditor shall release what he has lent to his neighbor. He shall not exact it of his neighbor, his brother, because the LORD's release has been proclaimed. (Deuteronomy 15:1–2)

While this commandment makes no sense from a worldly perspective, God promised to bless the people of Israel tremendously if they would observe this law.

Jesus encouraged us to be generous in our forgiveness of others and to prioritize forgiveness always. At the same time, when Jesus spoke about forgiving debts in the Lord's Prayer, he alluded to the idea of the year of release.

The Sabbath day is a foretaste of the Messianic Kingdom each week. In the same way, the seventh year is also a vivid picture of the ultimate redemption of the world when the Messiah comes again.

We extend grace and forgiveness to others, releasing them from their debts to us, and we ask for God to be no less merciful to us. We ask him to release the entire world from its current condition of bondage and send the Messiah to bring ultimate freedom.

Lead Us Not into Temptation, but Deliver Us from Evil

The Hebrew word for temptation also means "test" or "trial." This term refers to difficulties that test our faith, such as the difficult choices that Abraham endured (Genesis 22:1).

This line bears a striking resemblance to other Jewish prayers. For example, one such prayer asks,

Lead us not into the power of sin,
Nor into the power of disobedience or iniquity,
Nor into the power of trials,
Nor into the power of disgrace;
And do not let the evil inclination rule us.

The idea behind this is not to ask that God will prevent us from encountering tests but rather that we will overcome them. What Jesus meant by "lead us not into" was that we not be given over to their influence.

Many Jewish prayers also ask that we be delivered from evil things, particularly influences that may harm us or sway us to turn away from God. Prominent among these is the "flesh," the animalistic and selfish drive within each person. In Jewish terminology this is the "evil inclination."

It is well known in Jewish belief that the world will encounter such difficulties and trials before the redemption takes place. These are sometimes called "the birth pangs of Messiah."

FOR THINE IS THE KINGDOM, AND THE POWER, AND THE GLORY, FOREVER, AMEN

Scholars note that this line does not appear in the oldest manuscripts. It appears to be an addition from an early generation of Jesus' followers. This phrase, too, has a common Jewish form, most likely inspired by the blessing of King David:

Yours, O LORD, is the greatness and the power and the glory and the victory and the majesty, for all that is in the heavens and in the earth is yours. Yours is the kingdom, O LORD, and you are exalted as head above all. (1 Chronicles 29:11)

The early Jewish disciples knew that the Lord's Prayer reflected on and sought the glorious coming kingdom of God. The ancient Hebrew prophets spoke about how the Messiah would usher in a time of peace, prosperity, and the revelation of God—the Messianic Kingdom.

Yeshua of Nazareth came proclaiming that the kingdom was near and would be revealed if the people would turn their hearts to him in repentance.

God is the true King, but his kingship is currently concealed. Instead, materialism, corruption, and death dominate the world today.

Jesus began a revolutionary movement of people whose citizenship does not belong to this world but to the coming kingdom. We refuse to bow to the current world's regime; we stand strong and wait for our King to arrive—the God of Israel and his Messiah—and reconquer what belongs to him. Today, just as the first Jewish followers of Jesus did, we declare, "Yours is the kingdom."